Our Senses
Hearing

Kay Woodward

HODDER
Wayland

an imprint of Hodder Children's Books

Our Senses
Hearing ● Sight ● Smell ● Taste ● Touch

For more information on this series and other Hodder Wayland titles,
go to www.hodderwayland.co.uk

Senses – Hearing

Copyright © 2005 Hodder Wayland
First published in 2005 by Hodder Wayland,
an imprint of Hodder Children's Books.

Commissioning Editor: Victoria Brooker
Consultant: Carol Ballard
Book Designer: Jane Hawkins

Book Editor: Katie Sergeant
Picture Research: Katie Sergeant
Cover: Hodder Children's Books

British Library Cataloguing in Publication Data
Woodward, Kay
   Hearing. - (Our Senses)
   1.Hearing - Juvenile literature
   I.Title
   612.8'5

ISBN 0750246707

Printed in China by WKT Company Ltd

Hodder Children's Books
A division of Hodder Headline Limited
338 Euston Road, London NW1 3BH

Cover: A girl listening to music on
her headphones.

Picture Acknowledgements
The publisher would like to thank the following for
permission to reproduce their pictures: Alamy/David
Hoffman Photo Library 4 (David Hoffman), 14 (Harald
Theissen); Corbis *Title page* and 6 (Norbert Schaefer), 9
(Eye Ubiquitous/Robert & Linda Mostyn), 10 (Jay Dickman),
11 (Richard Hutchings), 15 (Richard Hutchings), 16 (Nathan
Benn), 17 (Richard T. Nowitz), *Imprint page* and 18 (Royalty-
Free), 19 (Joe McDonald), 21 (Ecoscene/Robin Williams);
Getty Images 5 (Taxi/Alan Powdrill), 8 Taxi/Mel Yates),
22 (left) (Photodisc Blue/Royalty-free), 23 (Stone/Peter Cade);
OSF 20 (M. Wendler/Okapia); Wayland Picture Library 22
(right); zefa *Cover* (Graham French), 12 (Virgo), 13 (A.B./S.
Borges). Artwork on page 7 is by Peter Bull.

Contents

Words in **bold** can be found in the glossary on page 24.

Sounds all around!

The world is filled with all sorts of different sounds. There are loud noises and soft whispers. There are high screeches and low rumbles.

▲ Busy playgrounds are noisy places.

▲ Sounds go into the ears.

Our **sense** of **hearing** allows us to **listen** to the many amazing sounds all around. We use our **ears** to hear.

How we hear

Sound travels through the air and into your ears. **Information** about the sound is sent to your brain. This is how you hear things.

Try covering your ears with your hands.
What can you hear? ▼

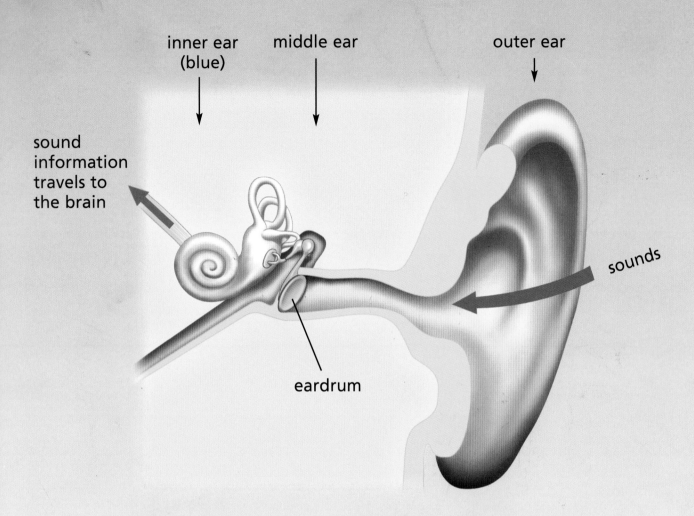

inner ear
(blue)

middle ear

outer ear

sound
information
travels to
the brain

sounds

eardrum

▲This is what the ear looks like from
the inside.

Each ear is made up of three parts. The
outer ear is the part you can see. It is
separated from the **middle ear** by the
eardrum. The middle ear and the **inner
ear** are inside your head. All of these
parts are joined together.

Loud and soft

Sounds are made when something moves. Small movements make soft sounds. If you hit the drums lightly you will make a soft sound. But if you really bang the drums you will make a much louder noise.

Very loud sounds can harm the ears. People who have noisy jobs wear **earmuffs**. These stop too much sound from getting into the ears and harming them.

High and low

Some sounds are high and others are low.
When people scream, they make a high sound.
When people snore, they make a low sound.

Singers use their voices to make lots of sounds, from very high to very low. How many different sounds can you sing?

Musical sounds

Musical instruments are used to make sounds. They work in different ways. You blow a recorder. You can change the sounds by covering the holes with your fingers.

You pluck or strum the strings of a guitar. When you press the keys on a piano, hammers inside the piano hit strings to make different sounds.

Hearing clearly

Some people cannot hear very well.
Everything sounds muffled and quiet. This
can happen when the ears are damaged.
Hearing can get worse as people grow older.

Hearing aids make sounds louder. They fit inside or over the ear and help people to hear the world around them more clearly.

Hearing aids can be very small. It is difficult to spot them. ▼

Deafness

Deaf people are not able to hear. Some people are deaf when they are born. Others become deaf because of an accident or illness.

Instead of speaking with words, many deaf people use signs and signals. This is called sign language. Some deaf people can tell what others are saying by watching their lips move.

Animals

Many animals have very good hearing. Unlike humans, they can move their ears around to pick up more sounds.

◄ Rabbits can hear very quiet sounds.

▲ A bat can tell if an insect is in its path.

Bats send out high sounds. They listen to the **echoes** that bounce back. They can then work out where objects are around them.

Minibeasts

Some minibeasts do not have ears on the sides of their heads. Instead, they hear through special parts of their bodies.

▲ The short-horned grasshopper hears through the sides of its body.

Many insects hear with their legs. Crickets have ears on their front legs. Some flies can hear through their feet.

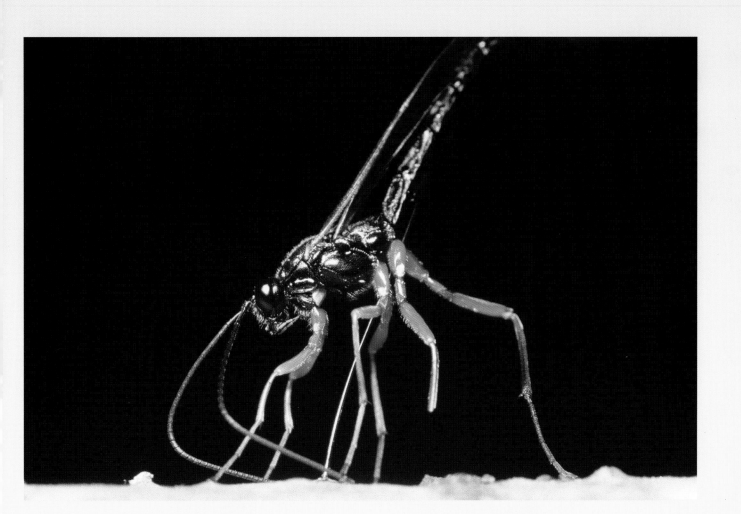

▲ This fly hears sounds through its feet.

Can you guess the sound?

All of our senses – hearing, sight, smell, taste and touch – tell us about the world all around. What happens when one of those senses disappears?

1. Cover your eyes. Now try to recognise different sounds just using your sense of hearing. Can you tell the difference between musical instruments?
   Can you recognise different people's voices?

2. Try playing Blind Man's Bluff. Tie a blindfold around your eyes and ask your friends to stand in different places around the room. When they call your name, point to where the sound is coming from. Now take your blindfold off. Were you right?

Glossary

ear   The part of the head used for hearing.

earmuffs   Thick pads worn over the ears. They stop loud sounds from harming a person's hearing.

echo   A sound that you hear again as it bounces off something solid.

hearing   The power to hear.

hearing aid   A tiny machine that is put into the ear. Hearing aids help people to hear better.

information   Things that tell you about something.

inner ear   The part of the ear furthest inside the head. This sends signals to the brain.

listen   Another word for 'hear'.

middle ear   Part of the ear that is inside the head.

outer ear   The part of the ear you can see. This collects sound.

sense   The power to see, hear, smell, feel or taste.

Index